Responsibility

By Bruce S. Glassman

With an Introduction by
Michael Josephson,
Founder of CHARACTER COUNTS!SM

Discarded by MVCL

JOSEPHSON
INSTITUTE
CHARACTERCOUNTS!

Produced and created in partnership with Josephson Institute

Special Thanks goes to the following people, whose help on this project was invaluable:

At CHARACTER COUNTS!:
Michael Josephson
Rich Jarc
Amanda Skinner
Mimi Drop
Michelle Del Castillo

Content Advisers:
Dave Bender, book publisher
Tracy Hughes, educator
& CHARACTER COUNTS!
coordinator for Meadowbrook
Middle School, San Diego
Cindy De Clercq, Elementary
School Principal

And thanks to:
Nathan Glassman-Hughes,
Emma Glassman-Hughes,
Natalia Mata, Erica Warren,
Ebony Sanders, Kellen
O'Connell, Nicole Rigler,
and Alex Olberding

Library of Congress Cataloging-in-Publication Data

Glassman, Bruce.
Responsibility / written by Bruce S. Glassman. — 1st ed.
p. cm. — (Six Pillars of Character series)
Includes bibliographical references and index.
ISBN-13: 978-1-60108-508-5 (hardcover); ISBN-10: 1-60108-508-7 (hardcover)
ISBN-13: 978-1-60108-509-2 (pbk.); ISBN-10: 1-60108-509-5 (pbk.)
1. Responsibility—Juvenile literature. I. Title.

BJ1451.G57 2009
179'.9—dc22   2008001192
Printed in China

Contents

Introduction: Michael Josephson...4

Chapter 1: What Is Responsibility? 10

Chapter 2: The Importance of Responsibility.................30

Chapter 3: Responsibility in Your Life.................................40

Glossary 47

Resources 47

Index 48

Photo Credits 48

Thinking About Character

By Michael Josephson, Founder, CHARACTER COUNTS!

Imagine that you're taking a big test at the end of the year. You really want to do well on it. You're stuck on a few questions—answers you know will make the difference between a good grade and a possible poor grade. You look up from your test and realize that you can clearly read the answers from the student sitting next to you. You're now faced with a choice. Do you copy the answers or do you go back to staring at your own sheet?

You consider the choices. You know that, if you cheat, you probably won't get caught. And, you think to yourself, copying a few answers is relatively harmless. Who does it hurt? And, besides, everyone does it, right?

Every day you are faced with choices that test your character.

So, what do you do?

Your honest answer to this question will tell you a great deal about your character. Your answer reflects not only what you know is right and wrong, but also how you *act* with what you know.

You are faced with important choices every day. Some choices are "preference choices"—for example, what to wear to school, what to buy for lunch, or what to buy your dad for his birthday. Other choices are "ethical choices." These choices are about what's right and wrong. These are the choices that reflect character.

Ethics play a part in more daily decisions than you may think. The test-taking scenario is only one example of an ethical choice.

You are faced with ethical choices every day. One of the main goals of this series is to show you how to recognize which choices are ethical choices. Another main goal is to show you how to make the right ethical choices.

About Being Ethical

Being ethical isn't simply about what is allowed—or legal—and what is not. You can often find a legal way to do what is unethical. Maybe you saw that a cashier at the grocery store forgot to ring up one of your items. There is no law that says you must tell him or her. But, is it ethical to just walk out without mentioning it? The answer is no. You're still being dishonest by taking something you did not pay for.

So, being ethical is about something more than "what you can get away with." It is about what you do because *you know it's the right thing to do*—regardless of who's watching and regardless of whether you may stand to gain. Often there is a price to pay for doing the right thing.

Character Takes Courage

There are many obstacles to being ethical—chances are you're faced with some of them every day. Maybe you don't want to be

There are many obstacles to being ethical. Overcoming them takes courage and hard work.

embarrassed by telling the truth. Or maybe you feel doing the right thing will take too much effort. Few good things come without a cost. Becoming a person of character is hard work. Here is a poem I wrote that makes this point.

It's Not Easy

Let's be honest. Ethics is not for wimps.

It's not easy being a good person.

It's not easy to be honest when it might be costly, to play fair when others cheat or to keep inconvenient promises.

It's not easy to stand up for our beliefs and still respect differing viewpoints.

It's not easy to control powerful impulses, to be accountable for our attitudes and actions, to tackle unpleasant tasks or to sacrifice the now for later.

It's not easy to bear criticism and learn from it without getting angry, to take advice or to admit error.

It's not easy to really feel genuine remorse and apologize sincerely, or to accept an apology graciously and truly forgive.

It's not easy to stop feeling like a victim, to resist cynicism and to make the best of every situation.

It's not easy to be consistently kind, to think of others first, to judge generously, to give the benefit of the doubt.

It's not easy to be grateful or to give without concern for reward or gratitude.

*It's not easy to fail and still keep trying, to learn
from failure, to risk failing again, to start over, to lose
with grace or to be glad for the success of another.*

*It's not easy to avoid excuses and
rationalizations or to resist temptations.*

No, being a person of character is not easy.

***That's why it's such a lofty goal and
an admirable achievement.***

Character Is Worth It!

I sincerely hope that you will learn and use the ideas of CHARACTER COUNTS! The books in this series will show you the core values (the Six Pillars) of good character. These values will help you in all aspects of your life—and for many years to come. I encourage you to use these ideas as a kind of "guide-rail" on your journey to adulthood. With "guide-rails," your journey is more likely to bring you to a place where you can be a truly good, happy, and ethical person.

Michael Josephson

Michael Josephson
Founder of Josephson Institute and CHARACTER COUNTS!

chapter 1

What Is Responsibility?

You probably hear a lot about responsibility. Different people use the word "responsibility" in different ways.

Think for a moment about all the different meanings you know. Do you "take responsibility" for certain things? Do you "act responsibly" at certain times? Are you "responsible" for doing certain tasks?

Being responsible for something means being in charge. It also means being "accountable." The term "accountable" means accepting the consequences—both good and bad—for your actions.

Maybe you're responsible for your pet. That means you are the one

Taking care of a pet is one way to show you are responsible.

in charge of your pet's well-being. If your pet does not get fed one night, you are accountable. If your pet wins a blue ribbon at the state fair, you are also accountable.

You can also be responsible for other people and things. Have you ever been asked to take care of a younger brother or sister? During that time, your sibling was your responsibility. Have you ever been given an expensive gift, like a computer or a scooter? If so, you've probably been asked to be responsible with it. That means, you've been asked to take good care of it, not to lose it, and to use it safely.

You Are Responsible for Yourself

Joan Didion, a great American author, wrote: "The willingness to accept responsibility for one's own life is the source from which self-respect springs." What does Joan Didion mean?

Didion is saying that one of the most important things you're responsible for is yourself. In fact, if you are not responsible for yourself, it is nearly impossible to be responsible for anything else. So, what does being responsible for yourself mean?

Most of us are responsible for ourselves in many different ways. We regularly brush our teeth, bathe, and comb our hair. Those are some ways we take responsibility for our own personal hygiene. We pay attention in school, do our homework, and take care of chores at home. Those are some ways we take responsibility for the

Taking responsibility for yourself starts with personal hygiene.

things that are expected of us. But you are also responsible for the decisions you make about your conduct and your actions.

You Are Responsible for Your Actions

Sometimes your responsibility is easy to see. For example: You accidently threw a baseball too high and it broke a window in your neighbor's house. You're responsible for the accident. Many times, though, your responsibility is not so easy to see. Consider the following story about responsibility:

Tad had just recently been transferred to Hillside School from another state. He was a bit shy, but he was eager to make new friends.

Every day for the first week at his new school, Tad ran out to the courtyard to find people to play with. But each day, he found that all the "play groups" had already been formed.

One group in particular was always playing a ball game that Tad loved. He ran up one day and asked if he could join the group. Gina would hold the ball over her head and say, "Sorry, no dorks allowed!" Then she would throw the ball to Cameron. After he caught the ball, Cameron would hold it out toward Tad. "Here you go, doofus!" he would tease. Then he would pass the ball to Margaret, who would look at Tad and say "What a loser!"

When Margaret threw the ball to MJ, he just held it. He felt that the group was being cruel. He didn't want to participate in the teasing. So, MJ passed the ball to the kid next to him and walked away.

Think for a moment. Who do you think is responsible for the cruelty toward Tad? Gina? Cameron? Margaret? What about MJ?

The truth is, they are all responsible. It may be that Gina, Cameron, and Margaret were more directly responsible, but MJ had a responsibility, too. He was responsible for speaking up to stop the cruel behavior. All he did was walk away from his responsibility.

This story is just one example of what personal responsibility is all about. As you can see, it is about being responsible for the actions you take as well as the ones you <u>don't</u> take, but should.

A Rare Public Apology

Indiana's Shawne Williams

Shawne Williams is a star forward for the Indiana Pacers basketball team. In September 2007, Williams was arrested for driving without a license, for having expired license plates, and for failing to signal a lane change. Passengers in his car had illegal drugs and an unlicensed gun in their possession.

The Pacers released a written statement about the arrest, which is standard procedure. But Williams felt the need to face the media in person. He wanted to answer questions about the incident so he could take full responsibility for it.

"To me, it's been devastating," Williams said in a press conference. "I feel like I let my organization and my teammates down, as well as the [owners] and my family." Williams also issued a written statement of his own. In it, he wrote, "I am very disappointed that I put myself in this position and I take full responsibility and want to be held accountable for my actions."

Williams's public apology was notable because he did not need to do it. He simply felt that it was his responsibility to apologize personally.

Now, think about your responsibility in a bigger way. What is your responsibility as a human being toward all other human beings? What is your responsibility to the environment? What is your responsibility for the generations of people who will inherit the planet long after you are gone? These are deep questions. And they are not simple. We will explore some of these ideas in the pages that follow.

There are 12 basic ideas behind responsibility. In many ways, they all go together. Let's look at each one individually.

Accountability

As you have already read, accountability is about accepting the consequences of your actions. It is also about accepting responsibility for the actions you don't take, but should.

Being accountable also means not making excuses or blaming others. A person of good character who is responsible for something—even partly—will not

Being accountable means taking responsibility for your actions.

shy away from accepting blame, criticism, or consequences.

Think about how important it is for others to be accountable to you. Don't you need to know that you can hold others accountable for things that are important to you?

How accountable are you to others?

Using Self-Control

Good self-control may be one of the hardest things we have to learn. For most of us, it takes a lifetime of trying.

From the moment you were sent to daycare or preschool, you were asked to start working on your self-control. What were you told? "Don't hit kids that make you angry." "Don't touch things that shouldn't be touched." "Don't make noises that disturb nap time."

As you got older, even more self-control was asked of you: "Raise your hand instead of blurting out questions or an-

Using self-control can often require a lot of discipline.

swers." "Don't use language that is offensive to others." "Don't eat the entire package of cookies for dessert."

A lot of self-control is asked of us every day. But we also ask a lot of others. We don't want to be hit or verbally abused. We want an orderly way to speak in class. We want the other people in our family to leave some cookies for us.

Using good self-control is a way that each of us can act responsibly around others. But, self-control is also very important in how you act for yourself. Putting the cookies away after a reasonable portion is not only considerate of others, it is also in your best interest. From a health and nutrition standpoint, it is the responsible thing to do.

Keeping your own health and well-being in mind is extremely important for maintaining self-control. It helps you make sound choices about sleep, eating, and other health issues. It also helps to guide your personal relationships. When you say "no" to a social group that uses drugs or acts irresponsibly, you are using good self-control. Good self-control is a key factor for success later in life.

Having Goals

It's hard to live life without goals. Goals are similar to dreams—they are what keep us going every day. Goals come in all shapes and sizes. Some are small—like doing an extra five push-ups in P.E. today. Some goals are huge—like finding a cure for cancer.

Long-term goals are the "big" goals you have for your future.

We often talk about goals in two ways: Long-term and short-term. Long-term goals take a long time to accomplish. They are often the "big" goals, like becoming a doctor, making the Olympic team, or becoming a famous actor.

The short-term goals are the things we can accomplish in the near future. Losing 10 pounds, making a new friend, or saving your allowance for a trip are some examples of short-term goals. Sometimes, short-term goals can be part of your long-term goals. If your long-term goal, for example, is to become a doctor, then shorter-term goals—like developing good study habits, doing all your homework, and getting good grades—are some of the first steps.

Most of us have goals of all kinds at the same time. Sometimes it can be hard to keep them all straight. And sometimes it can be hard to remember which goals are the most important. One of the best ways to make sure you achieve your most important goals is to practice good time management. That means being very clear on which goals are the most important, which are least important, and which fall somewhere in the middle. When you manage your time effectively, you work on all the most important goals first. Then the middle ones. And, finally, the least important ones.

Most worthwhile goals require some amount of discipline and hard work.

Another way to make sure you achieve your goals is to make sure your goals are realistic. That means, your goals should be within reach. For example, don't tell yourself you need to learn a new instrument and be chosen to play it for the Youth Symphony within the year.

Apologies Are Important, Too

An important piece of being accountable is apologizing for a negative effect. Apologies are good for a number of reasons. They show the injured party that you accept responsibility. They also show the injured party respect. Apologies acknowledge that the other party is worthy and deserving. And, finally, apologies often help to mark the end of a problem—they can signal that it is time for everyone to move on.

Think for a moment about your family and your friends. What does it feel like when someone apologizes to you? Chances are, you feel better. An apology from someone acknowledges that you are worthy of respect and care. It recognizes that—whatever happened—you did not deserve to be treated the way you were treated. An apology also shows you that the person who wronged you recognizes that it was wrong. Chances are you feel better knowing that the communication between you and the other person is clear. You both agree on what is right and what is wrong.

Learning how to recognize when you have wronged someone is very important. So is learning how to apologize. And apologies are not just for kids. Adults no matter what their age must know how to apologize.

Adult apologies are important on a personal level, but they are also important in business. Researchers have found that customers who

Knowing how to apologize is an important part of being a responsible person.

have been wronged in a business relationship are more likely to stay with that business if the offender offers a sincere apology. What's more, hurt customers are even more likely to be forgiving when a person takes personal blame for a mistake. Have you ever had a company or a business apologize to you for something they did wrong?

Setting and keeping goals in your mind, is an important part of living a responsible life. Your goals remind you of what's important. They remind you to think long-term. And they guide your decisions—helping you maintain self-control.

Choosing Positive Attitudes

Take a moment to think about something upsetting that's happened to you recently. Maybe you got a poor grade on a quiz. Maybe you didn't get a part in the school play. Or maybe you fell off your skateboard and broke your arm. How did you react to it?

If you reacted with a negative attitude, you probably felt really bad for a long time. Your unhappiness may even have kept you from getting a good grade on your next quiz. Or auditioning for another play. Chances are, the negative attitude just made a bad situation worse.

If you reacted with a positive attitude, you might have told yourself that whatever happened was a kind of learning experience. From that poor grade on the quiz, you learned you need to study more. From that failed audition, you learned that you're better suited to some parts and not others. From breaking your arm, you learned that skateboarding really can be dangerous.

Choosing to keep a positive attitude will help you make the best possible choices for yourself and those around you. And making good choices is a big part of living responsibly.

With a positive attitude, even failures can be learning experiences.

Doing Your Duty

Your duty is the action that is expected of you. It may be what is expected by others. It may also be what you expect of yourself. No matter which, your duty is taking an action you know is your responsibility.

Right now, you are mostly expected to do your duty in school and as part of your family. You may also be part of a religious community that expects certain things from you.

Self-Reliance

Being self-reliant really means being independent. A responsible person tries not to be a burden to others. That doesn't mean you shouldn't need or accept help from others, it simply means you should strive at all times to do the most you are capable of.

Striving to do the most you are capable of is very important in sports as well. So is proper goal setting. In most sports, you are not only competing with others, you are also competing with yourself. If you keep the proper perspective, you'll remember that—more important than winning every time—the truest goal is about doing the best you're capable of every time.

Pursuing Excellence

Being self-reliant overlaps with pursuing excellence. Just as responsible people work to best of their ability, they also always strive to be their best.

How do you strive to do your best? There's no substitute for hard work and patience. The first thing to remember is perseverance. That means "sticking with it." Most people cannot achieve their best all the time—or the first time out. People who do succeed are always the ones who keep at it until the best is done.

A responsible person always tries to do her personal best.

Another part of pursuing excellence is developing a strong "work ethic." A good work ethic means working hard, being prepared, organized, and paying attention to details. It means you stick with a job until it's done. It also means that, when your done, your job is worthy of pride.

A strong "work ethic" is one of the most important skills you can develop.

A good work ethic—and good time management skills—are some of the most important things you can develop for yourself. They are critical to success in all aspects of life. They are keys that unlock many doors as you grow older.

Being Proactive

Being proactive means taking initiative. It means not waiting around for someone else to tell you to take action. It means being a self-starter.

There are lots of ways to be proactive. Some are large and complicated. Some are small and simple. Helping to clear the table after dinner without being asked is a simple way to be proactive. Starting your own web site to help stop global warming is a more complicated way to be responsible and proactive.

Setting a Good Example

A responsible person always sets a good example for others. Setting a good example is mostly about having your actions reflect your character—instead of just your words.

Part of setting a good example is being a good role model for others. If you have brothers or sisters—especially younger ones—you have a responsibility to display good character for them. If you play sports, you should be a positive role model for your teammates. If you're involved in a school organization, you should be a role model for the other members.

Think for a moment about the people you look up to. If you're like most, you have a few people from different parts of your life. Parents, siblings, maybe your best friend. And what about your favorite teacher? Or your coach? Do you admire these people for what they say, or for what they do?

You may not realize it, but a lot of behavior you have learned has come from role models you look up to. And just as they have had a responsibility to show you good character, you have a responsibility to show it to others.

Good role models set good examples.

One Small Kid Made a Big Difference

Sometimes young kids take on very big issues.

Melissa Poe was only 9 years old when she decided to start a campaign for a cleaner environment. The first thing she did was simple: She wrote a letter to President Bush. Then she decided to do more. She got her letter posted on more than 250 donated billboards across the United States.

The positive response to Melissa's letter was so overwhelming that she started Kids For A Cleaner Environment (Kids F.A.C.E.) in 1989. Today, there are more than 300,000 members worldwide. It is the world's largest youth environmental organization.

Over the years, Kids F.A.C.E. members have distributed and planted

Melissa Poe (right)

over 1 million trees. And the organization continues to educate and inspire other kids all over the world.

Melissa's main message to kids? It's simple: "You need to start being a responsible, environmentally friendly person now. The environment doesn't care how young or how old you are, everyone can do something to help make a difference."

chapter 2

The Importance of Responsibility

What would the world be like if no one was responsible? What if the firefighters in your neighborhood decided to leave their firehouse unattended for a day or two so they could all play golf?

What if your teachers decided they would stop preparing for class each day and, instead, they would follow a random plan according to their whim?

What if all the factories around the world discarded their waste however they wanted—and without any regard for the environment?

Every day, we all depend on others to be responsible.

Industries must act responsibly to protect the environment.

Does that sound like a world in which you would want to live?

In order to have a working society, people and institutions must be responsible. Elected officials and business leaders must act responsibly and be accountable for their actions. Firefighters and police officers must be guided by their duty to protect. The principals and teachers at schools must also be responsible and accountable to their students and parents. When these people are not responsible—when they disregard their duties—the very fabric of a community unravels.

Responsibility in History

When we look at responsibility in history, we often look for answers to some of the world's greatest tragedies. For example, the *Titanic* hit an iceberg and sank on its maiden voyage in 1923. Three thousand people drowned. Who was responsible? The answer: A number of people, including the ship's captain, the ship's designers, and the individuals who equipped the *Titanic* with too few lifeboats. Determining responsibility for this disaster helped to make sea travel safer for others in the future.

Sometimes, the lessons of history are much less clear. In fact, the question of responsibility becomes especially complicated when we look at times of war. This is partly because war and the tragedies it causes often involve what we call "collective responsibility."

What Is Collective Responsibility?

Collective responsibility is about each member of a community having a responsibility to everyone else in that community. The community can be your home, your school, your neighborhood, your country, even the world. Here's one example:

> *You're walking down to the park when you spot a crumpled-up fast-food bag lying in the bushes. Someone has obviously disregarded their personal responsibility to put trash in its proper place.*
>
> *You pick up the bag and bring it to a trash can.*
>
> *While you did not have a direct responsibility for the trash being there, you did your duty as a responsible member of the community. You acted upon your collective responsibility to help keep the world clean for everyone to enjoy.*

Like picking up the trash, being responsible can have a lot to do with the actions you take. By the same token, however, being irresponsible can have a lot to do with the actions you <u>don't</u> take.

Being a responsible member of a community means, for example, that you are you not cruel to other people. It also means you don't allow others to be cruel to people either. It is part of your collective responsibility to prevent that cruelty from happening.

The Holocaust: Lessons in Collective Responsibility

Many times throughout history, collective responsibility has failed. Perhaps its greatest failure came during World War II (1939-1945). World War II offers a unique way to look at collective responsibility. The Holocaust happened during this time, when Germany's Adolf Hitler and his Nazi party wanted to dominate all of Europe.

The Holocaust was a planned extermination of all Jewish people in Europe. The Nazis mainly targeted Jews, but millions of non-Jews were also killed. Most estimates say more than 6 million Jews were killed in the Holocaust. Another 5 million non-Jews were also victims.

The Holocaust was not a random series of attacks from rebel groups or invading armies. And it was not limited to Germany. Millions were killed in Poland, Austria, Russia, Hungary, the Netherlands, and Czechoslovakia. Hundreds of thousands of military personnel, government officials, and regular citizens participated in the Holocaust.

And governments—including the United States—knew that such horrors were happening, but they did nothing for many years.

Even though the whole world knew the Holocaust was going on, most people did little to stop it. So, you may be wondering: How could such a terrible thing have happened? This is a very complicated question. And the

Adolf Hitler (right) and the Nazi Party ruled Germany during World War II.

answers are too many to cover entirely here. But we can look into some of the answers simply from the perspective of responsibility. The short answer to the question: The world did not take collective responsibility soon enough.

Background on the Holocaust

Adolf Hitler came to power in Germany in 1933. The Nazi Party soon became the official party of the German government. The Nazis governed through violence and intimidation. In a short period of time, the Nazis took control of nearly every aspect of German life.

One of the main goals of the Nazis was to rid Germany of all "non-Aryans." Aryans are a Nordic race of people, commonly characterized by blonde hair and blue eyes. The Nazis said that Aryans were the only "true Germans."

By 1940, the Nazis had successfully invaded many lands, including Austria, Poland, and Czecheslovakia. From these places—as well as throughout Germany—the Nazis began rounding up Jews. They forced the Jews to leave their homes. Railroad cattle cars began transporting Jews to holding centers, called "concentration camps" (because they concentrated the Jews in specific areas). The Jews were told the camps would be work camps. But this was a lie. Jews were brought to these camps so they could be killed.

The World Looks the Other Way

What did the rest of the world do to stop the Nazis from carrying out their plans? Very little. The governments of the United States, Great Britain, Canada, Argentina, France, Australia, and New Zealand were among a group that stood by and did nothing. Shiploads of Jewish refugees—fleeing death from the Nazis—were actually turned away at American and British ports. Horrible information about the "death camps" was received by the U.S. and British governments, but not acted upon.

Britain did not enter the war until Poland was invaded by Germany in 1939. It wasn't until the Japanese bombed Pear Harbor in Hawaii (1941) that the United States actually got involved in the war.

Nazi soldiers round up Jews in Warsaw, Poland.

Who Is Responsible for the Holocaust?

As we have already read, when we talk about responsibility, there are different ways to judge others. Some people can be judged by their actions. Others can be judged by their inactions.

Responsible for Actions

Millions of people—mostly Germans and Austrians—took part in the Nazi campaign to kill all the Jews in Europe. Many of these people were Nazi officials. But a great number of people were "regular" citizens. How did all these people take part without feeling guilty?

One reason is that the Nazis created a huge system that "dehumanized" the victims. The chain of command was long. And many people only carried out one small part of the total procedure. Some people only processed documents that identified Jews to be arrested. Other people only drove the trucks that delivered Jews to the railroads. Others only drove the trains that delivered Jews to concentration camps. In each of these cases, the people involved did not feel directly responsible for the eventual outcome.

The Nuremberg Trials

After the war, a number of surviving Nazi officials were put on trial for war crimes. But their crimes were so large and far-reaching that they could not be tried for one or two—or even fifty—specific incidents. The parts these officials played in the Holocaust were considered crimes against "all of humanity."

The trials at Nuremberg were important for many reasons. They held some of the top Nazi officials accountable for the crimes of the Holocaust. They forced these individuals to speak before the world and to admit their actions. They offered others an opportunity to somehow try to understand. The trials were also important because they set a new standard of responsibility during times of war. The trials established the fact that every individual is responsible for his or her actions, even in times of war.

Responsible for Inaction

Seeing the responsibility of the Nazis for the Holocaust is fairly easy. What is difficult is seeing the responsibility of the rest of the world. That is because the rest of the world was guilty of inaction. Why did so many seem not to care?

Many citizens in free countries were simply afraid to get involved. In America in 1939, for example, it was difficult for most citizens to get too upset about a conflict that was happening thousands of miles away in a foreign land. Many considered the aggression going on in Europe to be "someone else's problem." Still others comforted themselves by believing much of the news was exaggerated; Surely it wasn't possible that an established government in a "civilized" country was systematically murdering millions of people. "If it were true, someone would have stopped them," people said. No matter what the reason, people who did nothing ignored their collective responsibility. They had a responsibility to protect others and to defend basic human dignity. All those people played some part in allowing the Holocaust to happen.

Lessons Learned?

The Holocaust was one of the most horrific events in all of human history. But was it horrific enough to prevent similar injustice from ever happening again? Unfortunately not. Since World War II, injustice against many different races of people has continued. The world has seen racial segregation in the American south—particularly in the 1940s, 1950s, and 1960s. It has seen mass murder against the Kurds of northern Iraq in the 1980s. The 1990s saw genocides in Yugoslavia and the African country of Rwanda. Most recently, starting in 2005, hundreds of thousands of people from Darfur have been killed in the African country of Sudan. Many thousands more live in terrible conditions as refugees. And who would you say is responsible for that?

chapter **3**

Responsibility in Your Life

So why is it important to be responsible? For one thing, you expect responsibility from others. In fact, you rely on key people in your life to act responsibly without fail. Ask yourself: If your parents stopped fulfilling their responsibilities today, where would that leave you?

Responsibility is also important because it is expected of you. Just as it is with all character traits, what you expect from others is often similar to what they expect from you. Learning to act responsibly is at the very heart of growing to adulthood. You will only learn to be responsible if responsibility is expected of you. So, the next time your parent gets on you about cleaning your room or taking out the trash, remember that your

The more responsibility you show, the more responsibility you will get.

chores are partly to help you learn about being responsible. And, when you do your chores, you show others that you know to be responsible. The more responsible you are, the more privileges and independence you get. Those are some of the rewards for being responsible!

How Do You Learn to Be Responsible?

There are two basic ways that we all learn responsibility. The first is by learning from role models. Role models are responsible people we admire and look up to. When we see our parents, or teachers, or community leaders acting responsibly—and taking responsibility for their actions— we learn through example.

The second way we learn responsibility is by taking responsibility. This is also called learning by doing. The more responsibility you get, the more responsible you will learn to be. And how do you get more responsibility? You get it by showing others that you are worthy of getting it. The more you show, the more you'll get.

Being responsible is all about making good choices. If you know how to make good choices, the

We learn to be responsible from good role models.

responsible behavior will naturally follow. The right choice is not always easy. Sometimes it takes strength and determination to make the choice you know is right, instead of the one you know is easy.

Learning How to Make Good Choices

A famous lawyer and speechmaker named William Jennings Bryan once said, "Destiny is not a matter of chance, it is a matter of choice." He was saying that we have more control over our lives than we often assume.

More than anything else, your life will be affected by the choices you make. Knowing how to make good choices is most often the difference between being happy and being miserable.

Two Core Principles of Choice-Making

There are two fundamental principles that form the foundation of good decision-making. They are:

1. We all have the power to decide what we do and what we say.
2. We are morally responsible for the consequences of our choices.

The first principle goes back to what William Jennings Bryan said: your destiny is your choice. But what about when you feel powerless and out of control? We all feel this way at times—especially kids and teens.

Seeking good advice from people you trust is key to making sound decisions.

It's important to remember that having the power to make choices doesn't mean you have to make every choice alone. You also have the power to seek out good advice and to get the counsel of people you trust. So, part of making good choices is knowing how to get the help you need to make them.

The second principle is about understanding the full impact of the decisions you make. Every choice has a consequence— whether good or bad. And every choice affects certain people in some way. The people that are affected by a given choice are called "stakeholders." Most of us never even realize how many stakeholders there are for a given choice. Have you ever copied songs from a friend onto your MP3 player? Can you think of all the stakeholders affected by that choice? (Hint: It's not just you and the friend you copied from. Start thinking about the music download service, and the employees at the record company that sells the songs, and the musicians, producers, and engineers that work to create each song...).

So, thinking about all the stakeholders in a decision is one way to consider how important that decision is. It's another way of saying that the greater the consequence of a decision, the more important that decision is.

Okay, so now you know the principles of good decision-making. But the final part of the process is acting—actually making the ethical choice. Most of us know—most of the time—what the ethical choice is. The question is whether we *do it*—even if the consequences are costly to us or to others we care about.

Decision-Making Helpers

Choices are not always clear. Sometimes you will be pulled in many different directions as you consider what to do. Here are a few questions to ask yourself as you consider a decision. The answers may help to make the right choice clearer.

1. **Ask Yourself the Question of Universality**: If everyone made this choice, would it be a good thing?

2. **Ask Yourself the Golden Rule Question**: Would you want someone else to make this choice if it affected you the same way?

3. **Ask Yourself the Role Model Question**: Think of someone you know who is ethical and of strong character. What would that person do?

Building character is a lifelong process that takes courage, persistence, and strength.

Ethics Is Not for Wimps

Remember, being ethical is not always easy. It takes strength. And it often takes courage.

Being a person of strong character is not something that happens in a day or a week, or even years. For most "mere mortals," the strengthening of character is a lifelong process. There are always things to improve. Every year you work at it, your character will get better and better.

Ethical decisions can be difficult to make—and even more difficult to act upon. But great satisfaction and self-esteem come with knowing you did the right thing. Those positive feelings will inspire you to always make the right choices. This kind of satisfaction lasts a lifetime and brings you the most rewarding feeling of all: happiness.

Resources

WEB SITES:

CharacterCounts.org: The official site of CHARACTER COUNTS! provides information on programs, offers free resources and materials for students, parents, and teachers; also includes links to many other valuable and related sites.

Kidsface.org: Kids For A Cleaner Environment (Kids F.A.C.E.) provides information for kids and about kids who want to work to help the environment.

SaveDarfur.org: provides information and background on the genocide occurring in Africa, and offers links and ways to get involved and help.

NOTABLE BOOKS ABOUT RESPONSIBILITY:

Amber Brown Goes Fourth by Paula Danziger: published by Puffin Books, 2007.

Ereth's Birthday by Avi: published by HarperCollins, 2000.

North by Night: The Story of the Underground Railroad by Katherine Ayres: published by Yearling, 2000.

Moffats by Eleanor Estes: published by Odyssey Classics, 2001.

One-Eyed Cat by Paula Fox: published by Aladdin, 2001. [Newberry Honor Book]

The Edge of Next Year by Mary Stolz: published by Backprint.com, 2000.

Glossary

Accountability: accepting the consequences of one's actions
Ethics: guidelines about right and wrong
Holocaust: During World War II, the planned extermination of Europe's Jews
Integrity: knowing and acting on what is right
Perseverance: sticking with something
Proactive: taking initiative; being a self-starter
Stakeholders: people affected by a decision
Universality: applied to everyone
Work ethic: the discipline to work hard, be prepared, organized, and to pay attention to details

Index

Accountability, 10, 11, 17–18
Apology, 16, 22–23
Attitudes (*see* Positive attitudes)

Bryan, William Jennings, 43

Choices (making good), 43–45
Collective responsibility, 33–39
Concentration camps, 36
Consequences, 10

Darfur, 39
Didion, Joan, 12
Duty, 25

Ethical choices, 5, 46
Example (good), 28
Excellence, 26–27

Goals, 19–21, 24
Golden Rule, 45

Hitler, Adolf, 34, 35,
Holocaust, 34–39
Hygiene, 12, 13

Indiana Pacers, 16

Kids F.A.C.E., 29
Kurds, 39

Nazi Party, 34, 35, 36, 37
Nuremberg Trials, 38

Poe, Melissa, 29
Positive attitudes, 24
Preference choices, 5
Proactive, 27

Role models, 27, 42, 45
Rwanda, 39

Self-control, 18–19
Self-reliance, 25–26

Titanic, 32

Universality, 45

Williams, Shawne, 16
World War II, 34–39
Work ethic, 27

Yugoslavia, 39

Photo Credits

Cover: ©Bruce S. Glassman
Back Cover: *Girl group, three boys, holding door:* ©Bruce S. Glassman; *Holding heart:* ©Dee*/ Dreamstime.com; *High jumper:* ©Palangsi/Dreamstime.com

Page: 46, ©Rcaucino/Dreamstime.com; 44, ©Bruce S.Glassman; 42 ©Lindadalton/Dreamstime.com; 41, ©Lisafx/Dreamstime.com; 37, Library of Congress; 35, Library of Congress; 32, ©Oplantz / Dreamstime.com; 31, ©Otkr0yte/Dreamstime.com; 29, ©Trish Poe/Kids F.A.C.E.; 28, ©Artville; 27, ©Fotosmurf02/Dreamstime.com; 26, ©Bvdc/Dreamstime.com; 25, ©Deserttrends/Dreamstime.com; 23, ©Bruce S. Glassman; 21, ©Bruce S. Glassman; 20, ©Barsik/Dreamstime.com; 18, ©Razvanjp/ Dreamstime.com; 17, ©Vladacanon/Dreamstime.com; 16, Associated Press; 15, ©Bruce S. Glassman; 13, ©Tadija/Dreamstime.com; 11, ©Bruce S. Glassman; 7, ©Jimsphotos/Dreamstime.com; 5, ©Millan/ Dreamstime.com; 4, ©Josephson Institute